ALTERNATOR
BOOKS™

···TECH·TITANS···

THE GENIUS OF
TESLA

How Elon Musk and Electric Cars Changed the World

Dionna L. Mann

Lerner Publications ◆ Minneapolis

Lerner Publications Company
An imprint of Lerner Publishing Group, Inc.
241 First Avenue North
Minneapolis, MN 55401 USA

For reading levels and more information, look up this title at www.lernerbooks.com.

Main body text set in Aptifer Sans LT Pro.
Typeface provided by Linotype AG.

Library of Congress Cataloging-in-Publication Data

Names: Mann, Dionna L., author.
Title: The genius of Tesla : how Elon Musk and electric cars changed the world / Dionna L. Mann.
Description: Minneapolis : Lerner Publications, [2022] | Series: Tech titans | Includes bibliographical references and index. | Audience: Ages 8–12 | Audience: Grades 4–6 | Summary: "In the face of climate change, demand for electric cars is growing. Elon Musk founded Tesla, making a big bet on electric cars, in 2003. Learn more about Tesla's history and what it's planning next"— Provided by publisher.
Identifiers: LCCN 2021025729 (print) | LCCN 2021025730 (ebook) | ISBN 9781728440798 (lib. bdg.) | ISBN 9781728449555 (pbk.) | ISBN 9781728445281 (eb pdf)
Subjects: LCSH: Tesla automobiles—Juvenile literature. | Tesla Motors—Juvenile literature. | Musk, Elon—Juvenile literature.
Classification: LCC TL215.T43 M36 2022 (print) | LCC TL215.T43 (ebook) | DDC 629.222/2—dc23

LC record available at https://lccn.loc.gov/2021025729
LC ebook record available at https://lccn.loc.gov/2021025730

Manufactured in the United States of America
1 – CG – 7/15/22

TABLE OF CONTENTS

INTRODUCTION

The Tesla Roadster first appeared in showrooms in 2008.

It was a summer evening in 2006. The time had arrived to unveil Tesla's highly anticipated debut model: the Roadster. An airport hangar in Santa Monica, California, was decked out for the occasion. Tesla had invited more than 350 guests to the unveiling, including the governor of California, Arnold Schwarzenegger.

A reporter, Sebastian Blanco, was a passenger inside the sleek Roadster. Would this fully electric sports car prove itself on the pavement?

The driver turned the engine. He pressed the pedal. Zoom! Zero to 60 in about four seconds!

But there was no roar from the engine, no growl from a tailpipe (in fact, this car didn't even have a tailpipe). The vehicle zipped through the night, stealthy and silent like a powerful whisper.

Blanco was amazed. Tesla's all-electric sports car was capable of reaching 130 miles (209 km) per hour. On one charge, it could travel 250 miles (402 km)— all without noisily burning a single drop of gasoline.

Arnold Schwarzenegger was governor of California from 2003 to 2011.

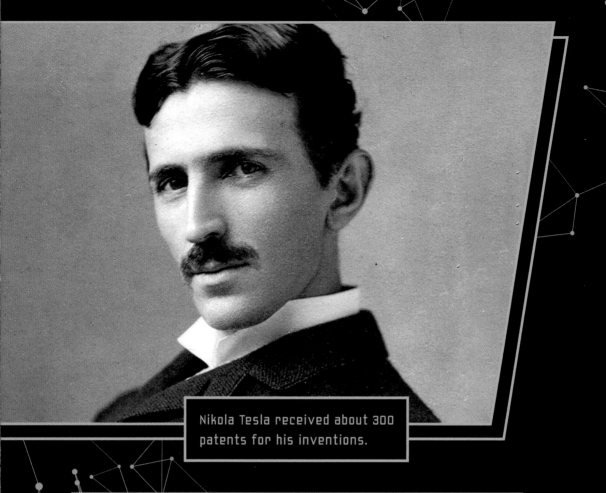

Nikola Tesla received about 300 patents for his inventions.

CHAPTER 1:
THE BEGINNING

Tesla was named in honor of Serbian American inventor Nikola Tesla. The company was founded as Tesla Motors, Inc., in 2003 by tech entrepreneurs Martin Eberhard and Marc Tarpenning. Tesla was in business to produce a gigantic piece of tech: a modern all-electric vehicle, more computer than car.

Eberhard and Tarpenning were not from the automotive industry. They were electrical and software engineers who had worked together to develop an electronic book reader for their company, NuvoMedia. In 2000, they sold NuvoMedia to a bigger media company. Afterward, Eberhard, a sports car lover who also cared about the environment, persuaded Tarpenning to join him in producing an all-electric sports car. It would perform with all the power of its gas-powered cousin without leaving behind a heavy carbon footprint.

Martin Eberhard holds one of NuvoMedia's Rocket eBooks.

BATTERY BUSINESS

First, Eberhard and Tarpenning addressed how to power the car. At the time, electric vehicles (EVs) had to be recharged often. The batteries were bulky and didn't have a long life. From working on their electronic book, Eberhard and Tarpenning knew lithium-ion batteries would be the best option. These batteries were lightweight, powerful, and rechargeable. Plus, their charge lasted longer than other types of batteries. To power a sports car, Tesla engineers would need more than six thousand lithium-ion batteries!

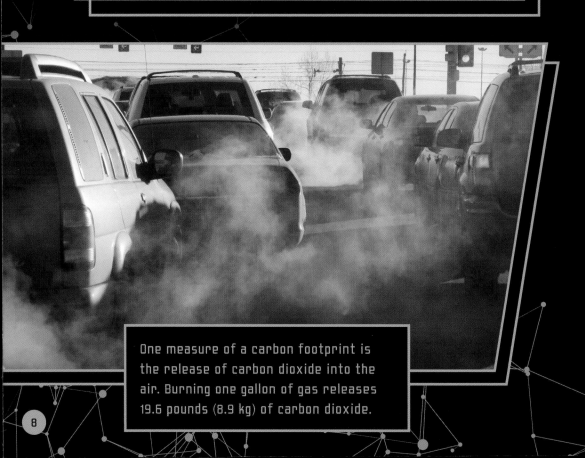

One measure of a carbon footprint is the release of carbon dioxide into the air. Burning one gallon of gas releases 19.6 pounds (8.9 kg) of carbon dioxide.

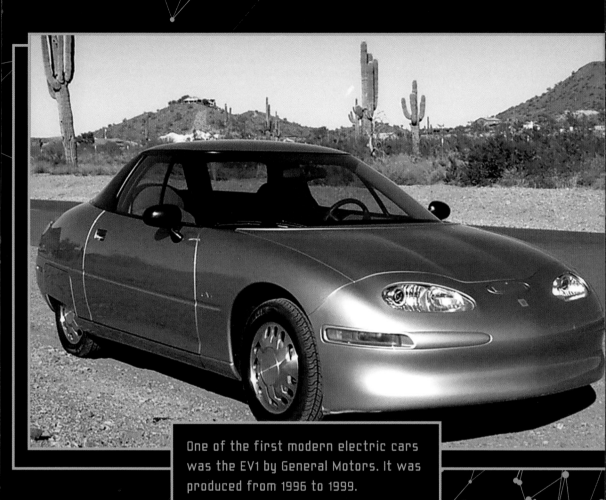

One of the first modern electric cars was the EV1 by General Motors. It was produced from 1996 to 1999.

Eberhard, Tarpenning, and other Tesla researchers conducted tests to figure out how to best assemble these batteries into a safe package for a car. Sometimes the tests got fiery. One experiment ended with a battery pack exploding and landing on top of a roof! But by 2006, Tesla had developed a battery pack perfect for powering its sports car, the Roadster.

Next came the body design. It needed to be aerodynamic, lightweight, and stylish. It needed to be safe, protecting both the battery pack and the driver in case of a crash. Tesla partnered with Lotus Cars to design the chassis for the Roadster's drivetrain. Finally, Tesla's engineers had to create the computer software to make all that hardware—the car—go.

Lotus Cars is a British car company based in Norfolk, England. It manufactures sports cars and race cars.

LITHIUM-ION BATTERIES

Lithium-ion batteries are used inside cell phones, laptops, and tablets. How do these batteries work? The metals inside—one of them being lithium—react to one another. This reaction produces a flow of electrons and ions. The battery stores the chemical energy and converts it into electrical energy. The 2019 Nobel Prize in Chemistry went to John B. Goodenough, M. Stanley Whittingham, and Akira Yoshino, scientists whose work led to the development of the lithium-ion battery.

A Tesla lithium-ion battery

ENTER ELON

Tarpenning and Eberhard needed to raise money during research and development. Early on, they approached Elon Musk, the founder of SpaceX. This company designs and manufactures advanced rockets and spacecraft.

Musk was immediately sold on Tesla's vision. He promptly provided funding, direction, and organizational support. Today, when people think of Tesla, they think of Musk. While Eberhard and Tarpenning have moved on to other ventures, Musk leads Tesla's product design, engineering, and global manufacturing.

Elon Musk

Tesla assembly workers finishing a Tesla Roadster

In 2018, SpaceX launched a mega-rocket, sending into orbit an original Tesla Roadster with Starman, its mannequin "driver."

ALL-ELECTRIC CARS

Since Tesla entered the automotive scene, other manufacturers have retailed all-electric cars too. Nissan has the LEAF. Kia produces the Niro EV. Hyundai makes the Kona Electric, Chevrolet the Bolt, and Volkswagen the ID.4. A Chinese company called BYD has also been producing EVs with their own battery technology. The Blade Battery, as they named it, is a small, fast-charging battery said to be safer than other lithium batteries.

The Nissan LEAF

The Tesla Model 3

CHAPTER 2:
STANDOUT PRODUCTS

After its unveiling in 2006, car enthusiasts prepaid $100,000 or more to own a Tesla Roadster. However, production was delayed due to problems with the car's transmission. In 2008, the Roadster finally reached the production line.

By 2012, Tesla had shifted focus away from making sports cars to making sedans. In 2020, the company delivered nearly five hundred thousand of their sedan Models S, X, Y, and 3. That same year, the Tesla Model 3 was the sixteenth bestselling car in the world. Tesla also sells a Model S by Radio Flyer just for kids. This mini-EV zips along at 6 miles (9.6 km) per hour!

The Tesla Model S for Kids

APTERA MOTORS

Aptera Motors manufactures a solar-electric car with three wheels, two seats, and solar panels built onto the body. With nothing but the sun to power it, the vehicle can drive up to about 40 miles (64 km) per day. Need to drive farther? No problem. The car's electric battery has a range of 1,000 miles (1,609 km) on a single charge. In December 2020, Aptera received over $100 million in pre-orders.

Aptera Motors was founded by Steve Fambro (*left*) and Chris Anthony.

CHARGED CARS & SOLAR HOMES

For its electric cars, Tesla also maintains more than twenty-five thousand Superchargers around the world. These are charging stations that operate much like gas pumps near major highways. Tesla drivers plug their cars into a Supercharger, and fifteen minutes later the car is ready for up to 200 miles (322 km) on the road.

In addition to vehicles, Tesla manufactures green energy options for the home. The company sells solar panels, solar roofs, and a battery unit called Powerwall. Powerwall stores solar energy to be used at night, on cloudy days, and during power outages. In 2020, Tesla introduced a lowest-price guarantee for their panels, encouraging US homeowners to go solar.

Early Tesla cars came with free unlimited use of Superchargers. Tesla later began charging a fee to use Superchargers.

SILICON SOLAR CELL

In the early 1950s, Daryl Chapin, a researcher at Bell Laboratories, was given an exciting task from the telephone company. He was to create a freestanding cell, or portable battery, that wouldn't degrade in humid climates. Up to that time, solar cells used selenium and produced little usable power. Chapin joined forces with Calvin Fuller, a chemist, and Gerald Pearson, a physicist. Together, they discovered a better combination of elements for the battery. On April 25, 1954, Bell unveiled their invention—a silicon solar cell. They used a panel of these cells to power a 21-inch (53 cm) Ferris wheel!

In 1959, NASA used solar cells on the Explorer 6 satellite. Four solar cell panels provided the satellite with power for months in space.

A house with a Tesla
Powerwall system

Robyn Denholm took over as chair of Tesla when Musk stepped down.

CHAPTER 3:
IN THE NEWS

With its innovative, eco-friendly products, Tesla was a news-worthy company. And as the face of Tesla, Musk was often in the news and on social media, building positive press and anticipation about Tesla's offerings. Sometimes, though, his statements on social media landed him in hot water. In 2018, for example, Musk tweeted something misleading about Tesla stock ownership. His social media post caused a stock-buying frenzy that made the company's worth spike.

In consequence, the US Securities and Exchange Commission (SEC) charged Musk with securities fraud. Musk had to agree to step down as Tesla's chairman, and Tesla had to oversee Musk's public communications, even those on social media. Additionally, both Musk and Tesla had to pay $20 million as a penalty. However, Musk still leads Tesla's product and engineering designs as well as global manufacturing initiatives.

Musk's troubles with Tesla and the SEC did not affect his leadership of SpaceX.

RECALLS & ESPIONAGE

In 2021, Tesla's cars themselves made headlines. In one case, Tesla had to recall 158,000 vehicles because there was a chance their display consoles could stop working. If that happened, drivers wouldn't be able to use the turn signals. They also wouldn't be able to access the back-up cameras or use the defroster to clear ice from the windshield. The cause of the malfunction was a flash drive that didn't have enough memory.

Instead of dials and buttons, Teslas have large touchscreens. Drivers use the screens to control the temperature, radio, GPS, and more.

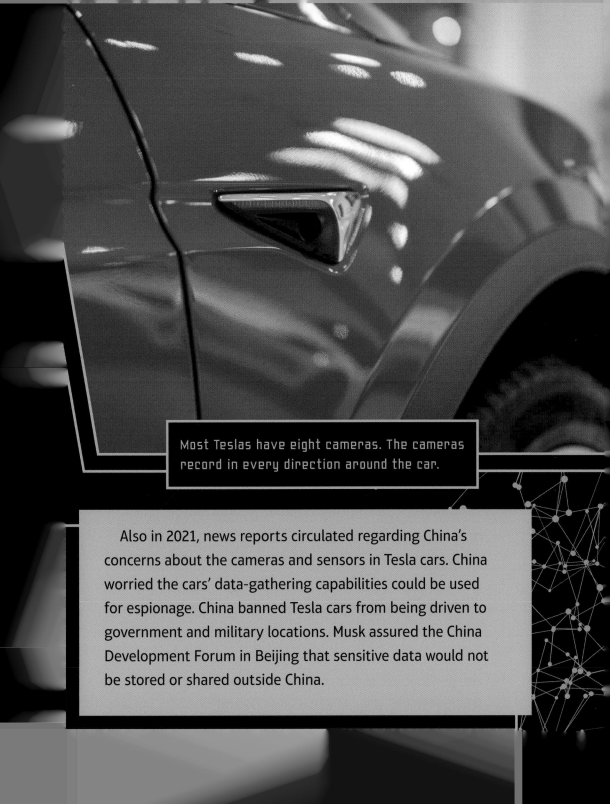

Most Teslas have eight cameras. The cameras record in every direction around the car.

Also in 2021, news reports circulated regarding China's concerns about the cameras and sensors in Tesla cars. China worried the cars' data-gathering capabilities could be used for espionage. China banned Tesla cars from being driven to government and military locations. Musk assured the China Development Forum in Beijing that sensitive data would not be stored or shared outside China.

The Tesla Semi

CHAPTER 4:
A LOOK AHEAD

Tesla always has new products in research and development.
In 2017, the company unveiled the Semi, a tractor trailer with
no need for gasoline. In 2019, Tesla introduced the all-electric
Cybertruck, a vehicle planned to have a nearly impenetrable
exoskeleton. And in 2021, the company was once again accepting
reservations for the Roadster, the sports car that started it all.
The improved model would be able to go from zero to 60 miles
(96 km) per hour in less than two seconds. It would also have a
one-charge driving range of 620 miles (998 km).

SELF-DRIVING VEHICLES

Looking to the future, Tesla has on the drawing board autonomous, or self-driving, vehicles. Imagine a fleet of driverless vans or buses moving passengers along underground roadways. Or how about a self-driving personal transportation unit? All you will have to do is get in, tell it where to go, and sit back and relax—the computerized car will navigate the busy highways for you. Tesla hopes to make this futuristic technology a reality someday soon.

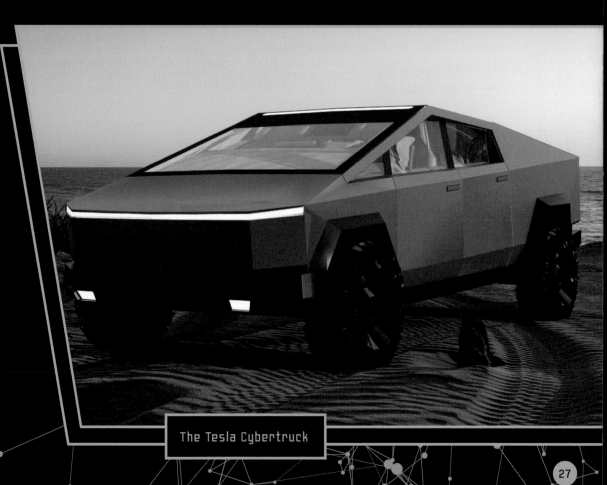

The Tesla Cybertruck

TIMELINE

2003: Tesla Motors, Inc., is founded by Martin Eberhard and Marc Tarpenning.

2004: Elon Musk invests about $6 million and becomes chairman of Tesla's board of directors.

2006: The prototype for the Roadster is unveiled.

2008: Eberhard and Tarpenning leave Tesla. The Roadster goes into production.

2009: The Model S prototype is unveiled.

2010: Tesla goes public and raises $226 million selling shares.

2015: Tesla introduces semi-autonomous driving through a new Autopilot mode. Drivers are still required to be at the wheel.

2018: SpaceX launches an original Tesla Roadster into space.

2019: During a demonstration of the Cybertruck's impenetrable exterior, the side glass windows shatter.

GLOSSARY

aerodynamic: able to move through the air with ease and efficiency

carbon footprint: the amount of greenhouse gases, such as carbon dioxide, that are released into the environment to directly and indirectly support a person's lifestyle and activities

chassis: the base frame upon which an automobile is built

console: the computerized screen that a driver uses to play the radio, see their backup camera, and perform other car functions

drivetrain: the system of components in an automobile that transmits the engine's turning power to the wheels

espionage: the practice of spying on a foreign government or a competing company to obtain sensitive information

impenetrable: impossible to pierce or break through

ion: an atom or group of atoms with a positive or negative electric charge from losing or gaining one or more electrons

recall: to bring back a product to the manufacturer to be exchanged, replaced, or repaired in order to prevent harm to the consumer

securities fraud: the misrepresentation of information that investors use to make decisions, such as making false statements about the value of a company's stock

sedan: an enclosed car that can seat about four people and has a closed trunk that is separate from the part where passengers sit

transmission: the mechanism in a motor vehicle that sends power from the engine to the wheels

LEARN MORE

Christensen, Victoria G. *How Batteries Work*. Minneapolis: Lerner Publications, 2017.

Elon Musk
https://kids.britannica.com/students/article/Elon-Musk/623517

Oachs, Emily Rose. *Tesla Model S*. Minneapolis: Bellwether Media, Inc., 2018.

Solar Energy Basics
https://www.nrel.gov/research/re-solar.html

Timeline: History of the Electric Car
https://www.energy.gov/timeline/timeline-history-electric-car

Two-Cell Battery
https://www.teachengineering.org/activities/view/cub_electricity_lesson03_activity2

Vance, Ashlee. *Elon Musk and the Quest for a Fantastic Future*. New York: HarperCollins Publishers, 2017.

Ward, Lesley. *Electric Vehicles*. Huntington Beach, CA: Teacher Created Materials, 2019.

INDEX

PHOTO ACKNOWLEDGMENTS

The images in this book are used with the permission of: © Frontpage/Shutterstock Images, p. 4; © Joe Seer/Shutterstock Images, p. 5; © Napoleon Sarony (1821-1896)/Wikimedia Commons, p. 6; © PAUL SAKUMA/AP Images, pp. 7, 13; © milehightraveler/iStockphoto, p. 8; © RightBrainPhotography (Rick Rowen)/Wikimedia Commons, p. 9; © Sjo/iStockphoto, pp. 10, 19; © Grigvovan/Shutterstock Images, p. 11; © Nick_ Raille_07/Shutterstock Images, p. 12; © SpaceX/Wikimedia Commons, p. 14; © VanderWolf Images/Shutterstock Images, p. 15; © y_carfan/iStockphoto, p. 16; © ZUMA Press Inc/Alamy Photo, p. 17; © ApteraMotorsMedia/Wikimedia Commons, p. 18; © NASA/Wikimedia Commons, p. 20; © RoschetzkyIstockPhoto/iStockphoto, p. 21; © CeBIT Australia/Wikimedia Commons, p. 22; © Sundry Photography/iStockphoto, p. 23; © Sjoerd van der Wal/iStockphoto, p. 24; © Stanislavskyi/Shutterstock Images, p. 25; © MikeMareen/iStockphoto, p. 26; © Mike Mareen/Shutterstock Images, p. 27.

Cover Photos: © Kathy Hutchins/Shutterstock Images (Elon Musk); © Sky_Blue/iStockphoto, (Tesla Gigafactory 3); © y_carfan/iStockphoto (Tesla Model 3 Performance)

Design Elements: © Hluboki Dzianis/Shutterstock Images